How
We Enter
the Palace

How
We Enter
the Palace

POEMS

Michelle Blake

GREEN WRITERS PRESS | *Brattleboro, Vermont*

Printed in the United States

10 9 8 7 6 5 4 3 2 1

Green Writers Press is a Vermont-based publisher whose mission is to
spread a message of hope and renewal through the words and images
we publish. Throughout we will adhere to our commitment to
preserving and protecting the natural resources of the earth. To that
end, a percentage of our proceeds will be donated to environmental
activist groups. Green Writers Press gratefully acknowledges support
from individual donors, friends, and readers to help support the
environment and our publishing initiative.

Giving Voice to Writers & Artists Who Will Make the World a Better Place

Green Writers Press | Brattleboro, Vermont
www.greenwriterspress.com

ISBN: 979-8-9891784-7-6

COVER PHOTO:
Sam T. McFarland

PRINTED ON RECYCLED PAPER BY BOOKMOBILE.
BASED IN MINNEAPOLIS, MINNESOTA, BOOKMOBILE BEGAN AS A DESIGN AND TYPESETTING
PRODUCTION HOUSE IN 1982, AND STARTED OFFERING PRINT SERVICES IN 1996.
BOOKMOBILE IS RUN ON 100% WIND- AND SOLAR-POWERED CLEAN ENERGY.

To Dennis, Sam, Katharine, Luke,
Augustus, Cora and, of course, Ralph

And to Garnette and Ellen and Michael—
this world is not the same without you.

. . . it's turning a little cooler, she is turning

She has given her purse of money
away, it's time
to turn back into Coyote

My, my Coyote in the doorway

—JEAN VALENTINE

The lesser saint

She sees things, this is her first
sin. She is early, nothing is ready, the grown-ups
fight in the driveway.

On the table an uncarved leg of lamb cools in the autumn air,
the door stands open. From the kitchen
a clatter of knives.

It is as if she has perfect pitch, words translucent.
She sees what people mean.
This is her second sin.

She is old as the mockingbird
and tired of her knowledge.
This is her third sin.

But from the tree of the knowledge
of good and evil thou shall not eat.
Who needs to eat? She knows

in her groin, in the sharp hollow between
her shoulder blades, in her body
so lovely she knew, she has always known.

CONTENTS

And in That Other Room,
She Said, I Will Be Able to See

Lives of Lesser Saints

Mariam of Nazareth

When I lived for a month in Venice, Italy, I got in the habit of stopping at every church we passed, a full-time occupation. Once I entered the cool dimness, I was drawn to the images of Mary.

Western tradition is not awash in compassionate goddesses and gods. Yet Mary shelters us under her mantle and whispers our prayers into the ear of God.

The Protoevangelium of James, one of the many apocryphal books not included in the Bible, tells a more complex version of her story. Her parents, Anna and Joachim, longed for a child, and when Mariam was born they repaid God by leaving their only daughter to serve at the Temple in Jerusalem until she was twelve years old.

According to James, she was sent from the Temple because she had reached the age at which she could defile the sanctuary, which is to say, she got her period. She was then handed over to Joseph, an old man and widower, who was instructed to watch over her and keep her pure.

One day when she was drawing water from the well, an angel came to her and announced that Mariam would have a child.

Of course, in this version also, she is a virgin when Jesus is born, and proved a virgin, because before and after the birth of Jesus, both the midwife and Salome check to make sure.

What are we to do with such stories?

Imagine that Mariam *was* a young girl on her own in the Temple in Jerusalem, hundreds coming and going daily, Roman mercenaries in the streets. It is easy to imagine how she might become pregnant.

In *The Gospel According to Jesus*, Stephen Mitchell writes:
If an angel appeared, he appeared only to Mary, and she was unmarried, and her too-early pregnancy was a scandal to the whole village . . . she would have had to eat derision and insult with her daily bread for as long as she lived.

As for the social effects on a young child: growing up with the shame of being called a bastard must be almost as painful as being illegitimate in fact.

Here is one possible miracle: a man in 1st century Galilee accepts a bride who is already carrying a child. And here is another: a young woman and her son spend their lives as outcasts and learn the lessons of compassion and humility.

Amid condemnation and cruelty, she raised a son who attended to the sick, the possessed, the poor in spirit and the poor.

This Mary, this Mariam, this mother and teacher is a woman of courage and wisdom.

Santa Maria Assunta is an exquisite Venetian Byzantine basilica on the island of Torcello. An inscription on the foundation indicates that the building was founded in 639, though there have been at least two major renovations, the last in 1008.

In the half dome of the main apse, an eleventh century mosaic depicts a monumental standing Virgin Hodegetria, *She who shows the Way,* an image of Mariam holding the baby in her left arm, using her right hand to point to him.

She is robed in blue and gold, against a gold mosaic background.

Under her feet is a register of saints.

It is impossible to stand before the apse and not be awed by her presence—guide and sovereign of that ancient holy place.

Angel of the Annunciation

Listen and be still
I am the hand of God and you
are God's hand. Its will
requires the two
of us and others. Alone It cannot
reach the world. We part
the seas and calm the ram caught
in the thicket. We bring low the high hearted.

No one knows this
or cares. Your son will be a thorn
in everyone's side, saying what is
and what is not. But he's small and born
on the wrong side of the blanket
so they may listen.
We will survive, you and I, both
invisible, wraith and woman.

Walk with the ones
who know—bondsman, widow, thief.
Go with him to the Road of Stones.
Abide. Leave
none untold. Remember
this—there are more of us in heaven
than your small world can bear
and we are women.

*Mariam speaks to her cousin Elizabeth, pregnant
with John the Baptist*

Before the angel, I knew—a quickening, yes
a fish

a cradle of moss, the sword
in the garden, the road of stones

What happened first was this—
soldiers came

they broke our water jars, they laid us down
in the dust

When the fathers wanted shame from us
I traded shame for peace

But my father turned his face
to the wall, seeing only stone

on stone, his hatred
for his own kind

What happened next cannot be made
into words—I say only

*My body opened. From the angel
I learned his name*

The fathers claimed
she made it holy

but, no
the child made it holy

He stirred within and spoke and I woke
wholly awake at last

The women knew, you, and the slaves
touching my robes as I passed

sweeping a path for me in the dust
It is always so—

their sins eat them from within. Only those outside
the rules can weep and know.

Elizabeth speaks to Mariam

My child talks to me night
and day, in dreams and in waking
of your child's nights

in the desert
He will abandon God. He will make
faith with Satan, choosing earth

over heaven. God will rain down
blessings. From this your son will learn always
to abandon his first desire. God will bestow

a second choice your son
must take.
He will say to all, each one,

Follow me. But none can. Only you.
He carries his death, a day
you must not do or undo.

All things pass away.
What remains?
Not the word *lord* or *king*

and not these ways. My son claims
this story we make today, this story
we have made remains.

Julian of Norwich

Though Julian of Norwich was the first woman to write a book in the English language, or at least a book that was circulated and read, we don't know her given name.

We don't know how she lived, how she was educated, whether she married and had children, whether she once joined a holy order.

She was born in 1342 and lived during a time of tremendous upheaval—the Hundred Years War; three rounds of the plague, which eventually killed off at least half the people of Europe; the heretical teachings of Wyclif and the Lollards, as well as the Avignon papacy.

It makes sense that Julian wrote during this period. The tremendous external pressures of plague, war, starvation and revolt produced corresponding, elemental shifts in awareness.

In 1372, at age thirty, Julian was granted an answer to her prayers for affliction and revelation. As she lay on her deathbed, her local priest performed last rites and held the crucifix before her face.

She saw the first of sixteen visions, beginning with vivid images of Christ's suffering on the cross.

At the end of the visions, she sat up, fully healed. She recorded her experience in the *Short Version* of the *Shewings of Divine Love*. But she was not done.

Over the next twenty years, she became an anchoress, walled into a sealed cell attached to the Church of Saint Julian. There she devoted herself to prayer and study and the writing of the *Long Version* of the *Shewings*, now considered a masterpiece of mystical theology.

After reading *Shewings*, I believe this is the true version of her story: she once had a husband and children and lost them all, which would not have been unusual.

The maternal is central to her theology, and she shows a profound grasp of suffering and the compassion that can come of suffering.

She records that Jesus is both Mother and Father to us all and that God is never angry.

She describes the Divine as *homely*, meaning comfortable, comforting, like a hearth.

She likens the entire universe, all that has been created, to a hazelnut.

As an anchoress, she lived in a single cell with no door and three windows—one looking onto the altar, one onto a hallway so that servants could bring food and remove waste, and one onto the street.

At this window, people could come to her for counsel, and she was much sought after.

After the cell was sealed, she never stepped outside it. Consider her other options—once again becoming a wife and mother or joining a religious order. Neither of these lives would leave her time to write.

The sealed cell was her guarantee, perhaps the only possible guarantee, that she would be able to spend her time praying, studying, meditating and recording the wisdom and compassion of the *shewings*, honoring both her visions and her genius.

And fifteen years after, and more, I was answered in ghostly understanding, saying thus: Wouldst thou learn thy Lord›s meaning in this thing? Learn it well: Love was His meaning. Who shewed it thee? Love. What shewed He thee? Love. Wherefore shewed it He? For Love. Hold thee therein and thou shalt learn and know more in the same. But thou shalt never know nor learn therein any other thing without end.

Thus was I learned that Love was our Lord's meaning.

i

Did I once lust and wander? Adventure lured
like a stag in the wood. Man can hunt
and do as he will while we must spin and care.
For that I now know I was not meant.
After the rack of grief had rent me, back
broke by my children's deaths, Our Lady, no meekness,
joined me in darkness, there in the dungeon black-
burnt and lighted my way with fresh sweetness
like smoke in the winter wind. She lured me then,
not men, but the tale of her son
once lost, lost to her as mine had been;
a taste of her own pain and mine was gone.
And so did Love come clothed and beckon me
to live, *Benedicite Domine.*

ii

Sixteen showings she sent, proof of such might
and homely grace and good that I did
doubt my wretched mind and sight
and sense, but would behold as I was bid.
A little thing, the size of a hazel nut
and round as any ball. So small
I marveled it did not disappear. What
I saw whirled with the ragged glory of all
the thunder and the stars. Ah, she said,
Milady drawing near, it is the earth
and all that we have done and loved and made,
the holy world to which we still give birth.
Mark well how bright she shines
for next to her the world itself seemed slight.

iii

"Let women keep silence in churches, for . . ."
For what, I ask, did she then fill my body
with these words? And more than words, such more
that soon o'erflowed the bounds of womanly
meekness, of which I now have none. They teach
of sin, of pride, shame, death, but Lord,
my Christ, my Mother dear blames none, teaches
but love. You wish me mum? I ask. Tell her.
Make her no more let loose the winds that shake
th'unfastened casements of my soul. Let him
not send more wisdom in that wind. Aye make
it stop. And I no more will sing this hymn—
Glory to Christ the Mother Mother's Son
who gather us to love and love hereon.

iv

*Sometime after 1403, the woman moved into a sealed
cell attached to the church of Saint Julian and became
an anchoress sought for spiritual counsel.*

They think I see their fates when all I see
is them, light and dark in equal measure,
at least in most. In some, naught but an empty
pouch of air and pride and that confession
rendered when they know not what they tell.
I have little sympathy. I am old
and growing tired of human souls that dwell
so much upon their saintliness. All souls
are loved by God, 'tis true, there is no hell,
and yet in truth I often believe there should
be one for these new Pharisees who swell
themselves like holy cocks, yet do no good.
And so in my contempt I fail my Love
who doth through love my bitterness remove.

v

On this my final day I take my heart
and offer it like sweetmeat on a plate
as at the feast we offer the first part
to Her, there at the head, who turns and waits
and holds out her own hand as thus, and thus,
a touch a mother offers her first child
when each one is her first. See! There for us
she stands at the far gate. Oh I am wild
with this new pain of roses on the skin,
and I am young, a prince, yet do I know
such meekness that will turn the outside in
and all the universes overthrow.
Here. Listen now. Such secrets do I learn,
such pain and such release, such mercy pain child man,
            such sky and ground, such
                wildness in my side, such mother
                    god pain mercy sky love
                        oh my heart doth burn

Happy All the Time

Happy all the time

Who isn't happy in spring? The birds
are happy because the worms are out.
The cats are happy because the birds
are out. The dogs are happy because
the cats are out. The children are happy
because the dogs are out. The parents
are happy because the children are out.

God is happy because everyone is out.

Look look, God cries to the person sitting at the right hand
this week—John Locke or Marlene Dietrich. *Everyone is out!*
Everyone is happy! And to think, God adds, with a slow shake
of that tumultuous head, *Your lives could be always like this if*
you hadn't blown it.

           Marlene sighs. *You never really*
understood us, she says. Eve nods in agreement and because
Eve nods all the angels and archangels nod along with her,
which creates a windstorm that sweeps
the golden refuse from the streets.
               When everything settles
down, God looks pop-eyed at being corrected.
               Darling, croons Marlene
and laughs that heart-rasping laugh, *No one wants to be happy*
all the time.

Trying to bury my half-brother

First, we dug a grave; regret and guilt our sharp tools,
    stupidity our long-handled shovel.

Then our father spoke a few words: *He was always asking for
    it*, he said.

Once we perfected the brown rectangular hole, we laid
    ourselves beside him. Not our whole selves: each of us
    slipped out of the skin of the part that had loved him, that
    had beaten him, that had tried to forget he existed.

We covered them all up. But nothing stays put in the earth.

The little selves climbed out—grey waifs, like the shadows
    of small children. They wandered the rough terrain of the
    world, searching for us.

They came to our beds and looked down, each of them,
    with pity, with ashes.

Our father cried out in the dark and clutched his heart. Had
    he taken a strap to his son?

But our mother entered the darkness gladly, like a building
    shutting down for the night. They could never find her
    there.

As for me, the grey waif lingers. *You were his sister*, she says.

Sometimes she raises her head and sings a hymn about
    crossing over.
Sometimes she slumps on a stool in the corner, and asks
    again, as if I should know,
Where shall we all go now for comfort?

for Roy

The incredible shrinking man

When we were little, he was big. After a few Scotches
he ballooned over the table, crashing into the chandelier

with its stylish teardrops, slamming my brothers
into the corners, crushing my sister and me

into the tapestry rug. By the time he deflated
china shards littered the yard. Years later

I tried to forgive him. We walked the steamy streets
of Houston as dusk settled onto the Gulf, his head

just at my shoulder. From his jacket pocket he flicked
a small switchblade in the gleam of a streetlamp.

I carry it all the time, he said. *These days you have to.*
And I saw he had escaped nothing—the past

lurked in the sharp-cornered shadows of bank facades
and the dimness behind shop windows.

After the strokes, he had to be carried up the stairs.
Not a problem. He weighed a few pounds, a few ounces.

We could balance him in our cupped palms. At the table
he would weep. *All this beautiful food. But who can pay for it?*

His last night out we wheeled him through the dining room
of his precious club. People gathered to greet him. By then

he was hard to find, an egg in a nest of blankets. *I loved
all your mothers,* he told us, tears streaming. Then he died.

Now I keep him in my pocket. Sometimes I forget he is there,
then I search for Kleenex and find him, smooth

as a button, whorled by time and sand
like a shell—and stand amazed

so much could be shattered
by something as light and flawless as a single human soul.

Birthday girls

Snow falling steadily steadily down
and the empty pocket of dusk
opens to darkness.
                    Birthday girls, these
were our gifts—the secrets of frozen
skies like the secrets of children, hushed
and breathless, caught
at the back of the bus.
                    Born in the month
when lovers quarrel, when the hermit
blesses her narrow bed and the farm wife
opens the last of the summer peaches;
                                    schooled
by the cold, we learned the cold—heart
of the famished child, mind of the once-desired,
with the faintest memory of warmth
like the sweet dregs of fruit in an empty jar.

for Garnette, 1951-1991

Things

Bed
A bed is not a boat or a car with an engine
but a river in paradise where, if you float long enough,
someone will bring you a poem. And you don't even
have to say thank you. That's how it works in heaven.

Window
A window is a promise cut into a wall.

Night
Night breaks the promise of window.

Cup
Hold out your hands. Together. Like this, fingers curved
   to form a hollow.
Now I will pour water into them.

Door
With a door, you never know.

Floor
The floor protects us from what lies beneath.
Sometimes it says, you will always exist.
Sometimes it slants or buckles and we see the truth
and want to lie down on the rag rug, however filthy,
and curl up to fit into its perfect concentric circles.

House with the black door
The house with the black door can never be torn down.
When we go there for services, we enter through the front—
wine & gladioli sparkling in vases.
When you enter through the back, it's a different story.

The inventors of absence

First we followed the animals through the wild scrub
to the upland berries, north to the cool springs
south to the succulent leaves.

We carried our homes, bound with willow
to our bent backs. Like the turtle
we were always *here*.

The young began to notice the way
the birds arrived unburdened just as the light
grew longer, how they fed carelessly

and left before the late storms. No calls at dawn
no long-necked dancers in the shallows.
But where do they go?

Rules appeared: *Everyone
must carry a house*. More and more
shadows slipped past

until when we gathered by the fires
at dusk, we found ourselves
surrounded by absence.

Ancient is the desire

*So ancient is the desire of one another which is implanted in us,
reuniting our original nature, seeking to make one of two . . .*
—PLATO

Once we were all, each of us,
whole creatures—four arms, four legs,
blessed by constant union
and the deftness of many limbs.

We groped so close to the sublime
the gods got scared and chose
to part us from one another, so that
now from womb to grave

we spend millions of dollars
and millions of hours in search
of our cleaved selves—Van Gogh
made do with candles

stuck to his brim and Edison
trusted in tungsten. While Proust,
could bear no illumination
but what the mind provides.

You and I met at night, in the mountains
among the stars, and the jazz played
at the club we'd left had been like light
itself, so it might

have helped me to see those limbs,
might have aided my split
and aching heart
to discover its other half.

for Dennis

Advent

After all, it was a marvel—
our baby on my belly,
quiet as sky, eyes wide.
Katharine you said,
and spread her hand,
a whole life in that palm.

Six weeks later she floated
on the shallow pool of sickness
like a husk. We watched her breathing
up and down, away from us.
On the children's ward the carols
wafted from the waiting room,
ghosts of the holidays—
we kept vigil so our presence
might pin her body there.

Midnight, my turn, the hall
small stars of light along linoleum,
I start to understand—spirit
made flesh, the miracle,
how we need it for ourselves.

Photo of Sam at the Pamet

In a huge sand landscape
a small boy
in black trunks
runs along the river
toward a white dog,
arms cocked like commas,
right hand, left arm
unfinished, no hand, only
a rounded end with tiny buds,
the beginnings of fingers, like the thought
hand that was never spoken in his body.

It was the summer
they laughed at him in camp.
I watched the boys slide away
as he came to them, again and again,
to show them his precious friendship.
Like fish in a school they disappeared
into one another—until
he stood alone.

And though
the tide is in and the salt river
fills quickly, coursing with
currents from the bay, and though
the dog is strange and might be
dangerous, might bite, and though
people might tease and stare,
still he rushes away from us
despite our terrible need
to keep him safe,
he rushes headlong again
and again into the arms of the world.

Visiting day at Heartbreak House

They look so nice, the moms in their bright
skirts, dads dressed as if to attend
a mid-level event; they thought about
what to wear, what message to send.

Thunderstorms threaten. A short umbrella
pokes from the bag of a provident mother.
You see the rest on their faces: what happened
to trumpet, curfew, the hockey calendar?

Visiting Day at Heartbreak House—
someone's son, fizzled at seventeen,
brain burnt to ash by meth; someone's
daughter on her third try to get clean.

In the hushed lobby they're handed tags
and passes. The women concentrate
on avoiding the glances of other mothers,
the men on getting directions straight.

Outside the clouds break open. The mother
with the umbrella checks her bag and even
feels, for a moment, comforted. Though by now
she knows any damn thing will drop from heaven.

Here is the river

Here is the river
in which I came alive.

I know there are many tales
of birth in the river—the dove

descending, the gray voice from the clouds,
the woven basket, the bulrushes.

This was not like that.
There were no witnesses.

There were the children, perfectly happy,
witnesses of a kind, true,

but wholly involved in their lives. As were
the gulls, intent only on water baring the shoals,

baring the sand crabs, the translucent
shrimp, innocent minnows.

There was life all around me—children, gulls,
terns, shrimp, each absorbed

in its business in the world—hunting, floating,
dodging the shadows, dodging

the light. And I, for once,
the water becoming

washing me bearing me
out past the jetty out

to the cold shock of the waves
to the sandbar reaching her bare arm into the ocean

was as I longed to be
wholly absorbed in mine.

My children float away

My children float away into the great blue sky
of the possible, where they rise above clouds
so dense and decorative
I cannot see their faces.

When they call I ask
Where are you?
You know, they say,
I am here.

But they're not. Only earlier versions
of them run ahead toward the roaring
ocean, the snarling dog, the road
with its monstrous traffic.

And without meaning to I call
Stop! So that they turn their faces
toward me and reach back for my hand
to lift me lightly with them into the wide and startling world.

Goldfinch, lilacs

Laboring up the steepest slope of the drive
I stop, still, paralyzed by shame
over a stupid thing I said decades ago
to impress someone who mattered to me,

not sure if I'm more stunned by the thing itself,
the way it has struck me dumb or how much I cared
about all the wrong stuff. I stare down at the ragged gravel
not sure I can reach the top when something—

a goldfinch—catches my eye
and I glance up to find the two bright lilacs greeting me
regal as queens, buds about to burst
into thousands of lavender blossoms

against an azure sky with a quarter gibbous moon
waxing to full. And see why the wise go on and on
about the present moment, which is, it seems, the only thing
that can save us from ourselves.

How we enter the palace

It is not about speed, the body
sees this, banging its shin on the fender
spilling white flour across linoleum

and the soul, wizened fig, big sister.

Not about rue, the shame you drag behind
in your wagon, the urge to pay back, to harm.

Each dawn a black shelled turtle, face
like a prize fighter, hoists herself onto the rock ledge
to dig in the narrow strip of soil.

Through the day I see her head
surface, sink
in the green heart of the lake.

This morning I find eight eggs, round
white syllables, lined beside the holes.

By dusk each one is crushed
In the dark, I hear her clamber onto the rocks.

My teacher says life is hard, and we must
respect the hardness, stand in awe of it
as we might stand before the great throne
of Vikramaditya

no hat, no shoes

but first we go slowly slowly
allowing the world to crack the cage of our ribs
so we enter the palace heart first.

Two poems for Garnette, 1951-1991

1

On the back porch
you took my hand

It was not a porch anymore
a small room with many windows

the children gone for the day. *I don't mind
dying,* you said. *But I'm going to miss you*

In the ether we come from, in that light void
we were together

In the cold white rooms of childhood
we were together

If we had not met in high school
in the high-ceilinged buildings

we would still have been paired
and all our lives not knowing who that was

who sat across from us by the bright windows, smiling
in tears, holding our hands.

★

2

You kept making plans—
a move, a marriage, even
when you needed a chair between
the bed and the bathroom.

One night, your troubled lover walked me home
across Washington Square. At a bar
he said, *You know, right?*
I ordered another glass of white wine.

The bar was dark, everyone young
and I thought of our nights at the Plough & Stars
the glory of you and me drinking Jameson's,
beer back, starved for love.

Ellen, Ellen, Redwing, Garnette

The air thins, molecules shift
to make space for us all
and the dead come in from the woods
Ellen, Ellen, Redwing, Garnette

They make sounds
like small pets, animals we have kept
through the years, mice working
to fancy my shroud

Without speech they say I will
soon be like them
entering through the walls
unable to touch the things I love

I breathe deeply and see the bright field of Alaya,
vast whiteness
abode of light

as in Himalaya, abode of snow

I Ching

> above CH'IEN the creative heaven, below CH'IEN
> the creative heaven
> *Thus the hexagram includes the power of time*
> *and the power of persisting in time*

The Quaker service in memory
of a friend's husband is simple.

We are silent. Only I hear a child
cough, someone whisper comfort.

When the first man stands to speak, he keeps back
tears. He has learned how long it can take to do

the thing that matters. He wrote his friend
a letter, too late; he had died that day.

A woman tells a story about a hat
the dead man wore to a dance—it had lights, and a sign.

I will always remember that hat, she says. Someone
says the man is with us still, remains with us still.

The man's two handsome teenage sons sit with their mother
and grandfather in the front row. The grandfather speaks in
   German.

He says his son was unique: there was only one of him. Then
   he weeps.
In my own mind are the mountains I have just left

snow glazed firs, row upon parabolic row
circling the slopes of the mountains, merging with mountains

beyond. The aged and shaggy ridges stretched away
from my daughter and me who had climbed for hours

to the lookout, taking longer than we intended; on our arrival
sharp light pierced the clouds and lit the valley.

You could almost believe it was heaven, she said.
I do believe that, I said. And this is heaven,

the man gone, everyone suffering.

Krishna fluting in the groves of Brindivan

Krishna spent some years
fluting in the groves of Brindavan

He opened a path through the round trees
with the silence between the notes

Water sought a new course
to be close. Clouds lowered

The mist lingered
and animals came

The old ways are filled
with these ghosts of beauty

If Parvati wanted she could break open
the world and start again, obedient

cloud and animal
but she is wise and knows

we must continue on
with or without such music

with or without such beauty.

Cave paintings

When we study them we slight desire
but people already loved the earth

the antelopes with their bounding backs
humpback bison, auroch

On the dark sheath of lime
they urged them, *Come, come*

Because that is what humans do

We want things

      ❧

Yes, they ate them
but first they watched them—frenzy of hoof
and foreleg, floodscape of sound and gallop
flowing away   away

What herds must have looked like
to limb-bound humans—

god, music

      ❧

Score of antelope, score of deer

How you make thunder on walls
lope and arc, lope and arc

In the firelight they saw
the animals dance

lion, bison, horse

Oh beauty, oh desire

Oh mind unfolding

In love with the walking

For JV

There's a sea you sail on
where I have not been—
galactic islands
blue-grey stretches of water

The space between thoughts

You are a book I can almost
read. Singing
leaving a trail of crumbs

Or surrounded by silence
walking ahead
nowhere
in love with the walking

I had misunderstood
what happens when we walk
to the far side of the mind
and look out—not the abyss

Blown leaves, lightning, red boat on a lake

already memory, already
now as it drifts over the water to later

You who forgive everything

four short poems for my son, the filmmaker

When I learned of your arm
forgive me, I grieved
heavy body, heavy weight

Then you were spark, rocket
tipping the weight of your own body
out the window

Now you go everywhere and your absent hand
holds a key. People give you things, ask you in, tell you
their losses

You who wear yours
like a bracelet of air
you who forgive everything

&

On the radio, Merce said, *Do it backwards,*
Jump first, then run,
even if it was just with his arms, when he got old,
even if some people hated it

—JEAN VALENTINE

You said, *I don't want to make* good *movies*
you who were spared the seduction of good
a part of you missing

I was not spared but am
old now, almost gone from the earth
so let's not straighten things up

See the world rocking its path toward evil
boats filled with the dead, the ghost of ibex
and dolphin

Now I think, like you, it is best *not* to turn away. *Do it backward*
he said, *Jump first, then run*
even if some people hate it

∽

The images you send, like glass bottom boats—
the door in the forest, unhinged; shadows in the slave's room
the devil's horses

They live in your head and you build them
I would like to walk around in your head,
calm the fear, feed the magic

but they are not separate, are they?
I see the fear there on the screen
in the doorframe, the slave's fan, the horse's eye

now as it drifts over the water to later

∽

When I think *you* I think
layers of boy. I think
smell. I think

shuttered heart
In your new life you are
man in a city, man in a garden

Where did they go
the long feet, the tears
at the edge of speech?

Man in a garden, man with a grill
man who stands square on two legs
man whose heart is no longer broken

On this day

for my husband, D, on his 70th

On this day the stars swim toward you
small stars, lights in a small city, swarm of innocent bees
a choir loft of voices
                        through the dark that has been your life
little fish in a sea of memory, what you have done,
what you desired once, desire still

They arrive in their ocean
of tides and fissures, treacherous
though neutral
                for the properties of force are neutral
mass of the moon, vector of wind, cleft
in the sand bar where the sea
must suck itself out to meet the sea

the force that ripped our daughter's fifth grade friend
from his father's arms, a small boy who played Four Square
and simple Bach pieces on the piano
his name is written on water
                        the same sea
as the warm salt glow off Zihautanejo
where we made love and our daughter
became an embryo, an egg in a nest

ocean where the ancient fisherman hailed
the albatross and Ahab's crew held steady
in *the infallible wake of the whale*
                        but today
you hold the key to this city of small stars

and the voices of the gospel choir of Jackson State and the shadow
of the ancient frigate bird float over the surface

over the fish and animals swimming toward you
to witness once again the near miraculous clemency
of one more year allotted a beloved human life

And in That Other Room, She Said, I Will Be Able to See

Catherine of Siena

In February 2017, I spent a month living and working in Siena, birthplace of Catherine and home of the Basilica di San Domenico, which now displays her head.

The citizens of Siena were crazed with envy and rage when Catherine was buried in Rome, so a group of devoted followers removed the head and smuggled it out of the city.

As they tried to leave, they were stopped, but when the Roman soldiers checked the bag, the contents had turned to rose petals.

On reaching Siena, her followers found that the head had reappeared.

This kind of legend is in keeping with many of the stories surrounding Catherine, who was revered for her austerities and mystical visions, as well as for her brilliant and tireless diplomacy.

Because of the Julian and Miriam poems, colleagues at the Siena Arts Institute urged me to learn about Catherine. So I visited her home, her head (mummified) and the point at the top of the steep street, falling away, where she first saw the vision of Jesus sitting in glory.

But the extremity of her practices—the violence, fasting, wounding—and of her visions—she claimed Christ gave her his foreskin as a wedding band—made me feel distant from her.

I was drawn to Julian's compassion and common sense, but I found little that drew me to Catherine.

Then I read that in her later years, as a teacher and diplomat, she always had three young noblemen as secretaries, and she would dictate diplomatic letters to all three of them at once—a sentence to one, a sentence to the next, a sentence to the next.

Her thoughts came so fast no one could keep up with her.

These were letters to religious and political leaders of the day—Pope Gregory XI in Avignon, Pope Urban VI, Raymond of Capua (her confessor), Charles VI.

I read more about 14th century Italy and began to understand the tremendous pressure her family would have put on her to marry.

One night in a hotel in Rome, I woke from a dream about her and said out loud, "Oh, she was crazy."

By *crazy* I meant *brilliant.* I saw not only the external pressures but also the pressures from within. She had a magnificent mind for language, theology and persuasion, she received divine guidance and possessed astonishing energy.

Her visions and austerities, the starvation and flagellation, might well indicate some kind of passionate disorder, but it was a disorder that allowed her, like Julian, to create a private life with no demands of husband and children.

The force of her intellect, slammed up against the stone walls of her life, pushed her to extremes.

Along with her correspondence, she recorded her visions in conversation with God, *The Dialogue of Divine Providence*, and in 1970 she and Teresa of Avila were the first women to be named Doctors of the Church.

She is a patron saint of Italy, Europe and the diocese of Allentown, Pennsylvania.

Also of firemen, because it was reported that when she wandered the streets of Siena in a trance of prayer and worship, she could walk through fires and not be harmed.

Angela nova, the angel of history

A child turns a corner onto a steep street
leading sharply downhill and sees on the horizon
Jesus seated in glory.

She refuses food. When her mother insists, she throws down her meat
for the dogs. Her beloved sister Buonaventura
dies in childbirth. She refuses marriage.

She practices flagellation and fasting.
She believes she must make herself
smaller than God.

Christ appears and takes her
as Bride. A married woman now, she can enter
the world of craft and gain.

In penance, she wears sharp chains at the skin of her waist
and refuses rest and sleep. She is seized by pain, then rises,
revived. We would free her

but she will not yield. At the end she receives the host
daily, living only on bread and wine, until
she can swallow nothing.

When we take her into our arms
she looks on earth and sees she has been not failing but fury,
bright ship, vessel of ardor, vessel of flame.

Catherine

I am Catherine but have three voices
in me. At first they had no names. I named them
Aldo, the old one who would wound my flesh,
Lupa, the she-wolf who silences me,
Sophia, the one who speaks through me but is
not of me. It is she who called
the spirit down to roost outside my cell
and led me to the garden, who offered my hand
to the Virgin and her Son, who bled
my father's heart of pride and turned him
to me, showed him the dove that
carries my prayers to God.

I am Catherine but have five voices
in me, the fourth my sister Giovanna,
my lost twin dead at birth. At death
she came inside and waited. She lives here
in my gut and twists it closed, tight
like a fist. She is perhaps the queen.
She would speak when I am silent. She would
pray when I would sleep. When I would rest
she works. To her the others bow.

Inside me a catacomb of cells,
inside each cell, a voice, inside each voice
a lamp that flickers in and out. I hear them
as a choir of flame. Each sings to me
a name, each sings a hymn, each knows
a piece of what we shall become.

Buonaventura, my beloved, suffered
the rack of childbirth for my sins.
I see her now a saint in heaven who calls
to me. But I had put her first and so
the old one, Aldo, wound me round like thread
upon a spool of love and stretched my marrow
almost to the breaking point. In pain
there is a sheaf of fire, a tare that blinds
me to the petty rest of life and lights
up only oh my God my God.

Angel of sweet truth

Her faith o'ertook her, the longing for all. After
she lay in trance, after she knew these truths
she concealed and then conceded, her other
angels, demons of woe, fought and grew
strong within her. It was not choice. Do not
think it was choice. The human frame has
limits—knowledge and woe have none. A daughter
of Eden, even, breaks beneath them as
she did. The fasting. The sores. Who else
has taken Christ inside, bridegroom and heaven,
what human form has housed him, what self
survived such passion?
Do not say *not* and *should not*
have offered herself, you who do not and can not.

Helen Keller

Keller was born in Tuscumbia, Alabama in June of 1880.

Her mother was her father's second wife, and much younger, fastidious and repelled by unpleasant or difficult things. Helen was her first child.

For a year and a half, the baby was bright and precocious, speaking at around six months and walking on her birthday.

The family lived in a two-room summer house, separate from the main house, covered in vines of honeysuckle, clematis and jasmine, in the midst of an expansive garden. Her father was a newspaper editor, outgoing and garrulous, a great lover of dogs and hunting.

When Helen was nineteen months old, she became ill with a very high fever. The doctor called it "acute congestion of the stomach and brain." Congestion was a common medical term back then, for everything from head colds to cancer.

Most likely she contracted cholera or meningitis, both of which can cause raging fevers, high enough to damage neurons in the brain.

In later books, dictated to her teacher and companion Anne Sullivan, Keller recalls certain sensations from this period. In *Teacher*, she separates herself (the mature writer) from that child without language, referring to the child in the third person, as Phantom.

Helplessly the family witnessed the baffled intelligence as Phantom's hands stretched out to feel the shapes which she could reach but which meant nothing to her . . .

That child did eventually create as many as sixty gestures, made with body and hands, which allowed her to communicate basic questions and needs. Slicing a loaf and spreading butter meant she wanted bread. Putting on glasses meant she wanted her father.

Her desire to understand and be understood became a powerful drive, reducing her to fits of rage and frustration.

Her mother's dread of scenes meant no one was allowed to discipline or contain her, which must have been doubly terrifying for the child.

Her frustrations grew. Her inability to articulate nuance made many feelings mysterious and even unavailable.

Thus it is, when we walk in the valley of twofold solitude we know little of the tender affections that grow out of endearing words and actions and companionship.

The fits and rages increased, with sometimes as many as one an hour.

Her single-minded drive to acquire language was her salvation. If she had been a docile child, making do with hand gestures, her parents would most likely have let her continue as she was.

She could fold clothes and help in the kitchen, feed the chickens, greet guests.

But she refused that life the only way she could—by kicking, biting, scratching and hurling herself to the floor. Once an hour.

Her father learned of Dr. Chisholm, an oculist who was having success operating on those who had lost their sight. He made an appointment and the family traveled by train.

Chisholm could do nothing, but he sent them to Alexander Graham Bell, and that is the visit Helen remembers.

He held me on his knee while I examined his watch, and he made it strike for me. He understood my signs, and I knew it and loved him at once.

(It's worth noting here that Bell's own wife was hearing impaired and unable to speak, but he refused to let her learn sign language. Among other objections, he believed it would lead to the deaf marrying the deaf and creating a "deaf race." He was committed to eugenics. He believed that language needed to be controlled and kept pure. Nothing is simple.)

At the end of his meeting with the Kellers, he advised them to write to Mr. Anagnos, director of the Perkins Institute for the Blind in Boston, to ask if he knew of a teacher able and willing to come to Alabama to educate Helen.

Mr. Keller wrote as soon as he arrived home, and Mr. Anagnos wrote back a few weeks later to let them know he had found someone suitable, a young woman named Anne Sullivan, who was partially blind herself.

Sullivan recognized from the start that Helen was able to learn. She began immediately to spell words into the girl's hand.

Helen learned quickly how to spell the words, but she could not, at first, connect them with the objects they named. They had no meaning for her.

Then one day in the pump house, Sullivan let water pour over Helen's arm and spelled w-a-t-e-r into her hand, again and again. And the child rediscovered language.

Sullivan remained with Keller, as teacher and companion, until Sullivan's death in 1936.

Keller then had two additional companions who escorted her on her travels, took dictation and helped in her home.

I first became interested in Keller when I read the note about her at the back of Anne Michaels's glorious book *Correspondences*:

> Helen Keller was a radical socialist, a pacifist, and a suffragist. Her work, along with the works of Einstein, Kafka, Brod, and thousands of others, were banned and burned in the infamous book burnings of May 10, 1933, in Germany. Keller believed that death was like passing from one room to another. And in that other room, she said, "I will be able to see."

A few impressions stand out vividly from the first year of my life . . .

Angels high in the corners. Light

         pouring through them, in through them

A square in the wall where the sky falls into the room each day

         and the room pours back into the dark yard

She comes and goes, comes and goes, swelling and sinking

         eyes, mouth, song floating over me

And the others, small drums, big drums on the floor

         the loud voice leaves with his hat

In the yard, a chicken, a gate, a star

         the dog lies still in the sun. *Gentle, gentle*, she says

Tea, I say. They all turn to see me. *Tea*, I say louder

         meaning the world

I fancy I still have confused recollections of that illness.

Someone is running, drumming. A tight hot swell

                that burns

I turn to the wall. My head keeps falling

Light is a knife, light

               is a hot cup

The room goes in and out

Someone calls my name outside

                  running and running away

Someone calls my name through rain

Hands and skin. My hair, my teeth.
Big drum, Poppa. Little drum, Momma, earth, body

Cloth cold legs. My skin. My mouth
Cold cup. Hot cup. Cold cloth

Body, Momma, what
she is holding, sharp as a star

What she is doing
back and forth, back and forth

Hot cup. Tea
Cold cup. Water

I cannot recall what happened during the first months
after my illness.

Lockbox   Wood   Brick   Block

A hole in my head where words fall out

There are my hands

           and the hammer that is my mind

                  knocking on air

I know when Momma moves

         the smell and silk of her leaving

                cold pouring in

Everything settles into my hands

         that can shape only lack—

                bread go come eat no

I am will

I make bird nest, they give me cup

I make cut, they give me scissors   I mangle the jasmine

That is not what I want

I cannot make what I want

Red is my pet. Red is my only—

hurling the world away

Red sets a fire in my head

If I tear at my hair

someone touches me

and the house returns

> *Many incidents of those early years are fixed in*
> *my memory, isolated, but clear and distinct, making*
> *my sense of that silent, aimless, dayless life all the*
> *more intense.*

On good days the boxwood leads me all the way to the
    summer house—
I know the smell of jasmine but not the name—*star? feather?*

Lily is the memory of song
The rose a mouth, a kiss

Outside the angels high in my head,
trees with wings

More words leave

Walls disappear
No one can tell me *no*

I am nothing
poured into nothing

Water is always with me

        cold as a saw

                a sound my mouth knows

Momma has company
I touch their lips, touch my lips
move my lips
move my arms, make
the gestures of women

pin a veil to my head
powder my face

and enter the long hall of *wait*

the body blameless
flailing its white arms

Momma can soothe me
No one else

Her body says *there*
Her body says *stop*

IF I STOP WE WOULD STOP
WE WOULD NEVER
                    GO
IF I STOP SHE WOULD
STOP IF I STOP   THE BODY
WOULD BREAK ITSELF
INTO BEES   ROCKS
FRACTURES OF GLASS

When I was about six years old, my
father heard of an eminent oculist in Baltimore . . .

we are all here and moving
the wheels underneath grind corn
a man with buttons, hole punch
we move fast and through
I touch the glass
underneath the gravel says
something says
going says going says going

in a tall place I sit on a man's lap,
feel his heart through the new cloth of his coat,
hold his watch, my sister,
touch my hands to his face, rough board

my body calms like a cake
the man holds on a plate

a woman walks on the porch

she has sweets in a trunk

she walks in my palm

she walks in my palm

morning, long walk

evening, soft walk

my palm wakes

the woman makes *no*

the woman makes *stop*

she throws herself into my hands

we are one thing

we are a long time

she is the last one

we are two things

there is this woman

there is this girl

Because I knew it
because it was in my mouth, a bird
                        waiting to free itself

because it had never left me
because the dancing tapping grappling
                        in my palm meant nothing until

it did until we entered the pump house
and soaked my sleeve
                        and the word that had never left

flew out and into the tree that spread its wings of green leaves
when the jasmine
                        raised its head of curls

because floor-apple
bird-tree gate-stop fur-dog wall-cow
                        chicken chicken

steps stars because cup-hot-hand because
cold-cup hot-cup tea
                        because *tea*

I make the word and they turn to me
Tea I make, meaning
                        the world

ACKNOWLEDGMENTS

Thanks to the Vermont Studio Center and the Siena Art Institute, where many of these poems were written.

The following poems appeared in *Into the Wide and Startling World*, a chapbook published in the New Women's Voices series, Finishing Line, 2012: "Ancient is the desire," "Advent," "Photo of Sam at the Pamet," "Here is the river," "My children float away."

"The inventors of absence" and "My children float away" appeared in *Escape Artist*, a collaboration with the photomontage artist Fran Forman, Schiffer, 2014.

"Cave paintings" appeared in *Cider Press Review* in the April 2020 issue.

Mezzo Cammin published four of the "Julian of Norwich" sonnets, the "Mariam of Nazareth" poems and the "Catherine of Siena" poems.

"In love with the walking" and "The incredible shrinking man" appeared in *Prairie Schooner* in December 2020.

"How we enter the palace" appeared in the Winter 2021 issue of *Asheville Poetry Review,* and appears as well as in a collection of poems by Vermont poets, *Time Capsule*, letterpress printed by hand, sponsored by the Putney Public Library.

"Inventors of Absence" and "Trying to Bury My Half-Brother" appeared in *Last Stanza Poetry Journal #7*.

Profound gratitude to Katharine Blake McGowan and Sam McFarland, my children, my guides, my editors; and to Lukas and Augustus and Cora McGowan, who have brought so much love and wisdom to our family; and to Clarissa Atkinson, indispensable friend and reader; to Catherine MacDonald, who kept making these poems better; to my agent, Gail Hochman, whose savvy, talent and loyalty started it all and kept it going; and to Robin Meyers, Kate Powers, Adam Dalva, Natasha Naayem and especially Liza Cochran, for flash workshops that changed my work and life.

And thank you to my husband, Dennis McFarland, for all the hours of reading and responding and being diplomatically right, and for all the years we have done this work side by side and kept each other company in the moments of despair and the days of celebration. May our celebrations continue to the end.

While I was finishing this book, my dear friend Michael Downing died. I could not have written this book, or anything else I wrote in the last twenty years, without him. I have not yet learned how to be in this world where he is missing.

I would also like to acknowledge the influence of the work and life of Jean Valentine. Hers are the poems I wish I had written.